Praise

Arisa White ups the ante with this bold and visceral collection of striking lyrics, bold and honest. It's a kind of song, truth be told, and these poems truth indeed be tolled. —**Kazim Ali,** *Sky Ward*

Whether remembering a neglected friend or experiencing a sensual touch, Arisa White's poems will take your breath away. They nestle into rich language then burst up and out like birds taking flight; so close you feel their heat and wings inside you. She traverses many landscapes, both physical and emotional, sometimes evoking a melancholy longing, at other times an eager passion. In either case, these are exquisite, finely crafted poems that are irresistible. —**Jewelle Gomez,** *The Gilda Stories: Expanded 25th Anniversary Edition*

This is what I'm talking about. The fierce truth, the gorgeous loneliness, the late-night bravery and the tender, tender heart. It's the poetry of Arisa White and it's divine in every sense. Let's all talk about it. —**Daniel Handler,** *Lemony Snicket's A Series of Unfortunate Events*

Arisa White's smart, angular, precocious and sexy third collection is filled with lithe anecdotes and disturbed resonances of how to negotiate a full life in everyday environs. These crafted, knowing poems put us in the middle of the room of living a realized, intelligent life of the senses. White's attentive word substitutions and range of organized forms refreshes the reader at each page. To live freely, observantly as a politically astute, sensually perceptive Queer Black woman is to be risk taker, at risk, a perceived danger to others and even dangerous to/as oneself. White writes: *I shake this heart to get the last coin out, the last folded bill where you wrote "Do Not Spend."* We feel that last coin drop, like the last mic of the MC. Throwing her caution to the wind, you *should* spend: spend *time* with the tender exchanges in these poetic jewels. —**Tracie Morris,** *handholding: 5 kinds*

You're the Most Beautiful
Thing That Happened

Arisa White

Augury Books
New York, New York

You're the Most Beautiful Thing That Happened
© 2016 Arisa White

ISBN-13: 978-0-9887355-7-6

Cover Design by Michael Miller

Published in the United States of America by Augury Books. All rights reserved. For reproduction inquiries or other information, please visit AuguryBooks.com.

First Edition

Contents

Introduction   9

Tail   11
Six Colors   12
With Feathers   13
Paw   15
Who Invited the Monkey To Omen's Party?   16
Auntie   17
Drag Up   18
Inconvenient Roof   19
Left   20
Strangers   21
Dagger   22
Lilla, Inscribed   23
Torn   26
Gun(n)   27
Trip the Light Fantastic   29
Blue Boy   30
Bat   31
Whole Lot of Lot   32
Warm Water   33
Dirty Fruit   35
Passing   36
Comrades   38
Little Deer   43
Chance Is Based on True Events   44
Hold Your Part of a Deal   45

Effluvium   47

Kokobar   58
Lady In the House: Kitchen Speeches   63
Mashing Cookies   67
Pedal   68
Four Square   71

Queen   72
Rooster   73
Beechnut   74
Glass   75
Closet Case   76
Craves   78
Manly Shoes   80
After Watching Obama Win His
    First Presidency, We Go See Tina Tuna   82

Seven Marys   83

Notes   92
Acknowledgments   95

Introduction

In May 2009, I came across a "List of terms for gay in different languages" on Wikipedia. I'm sure the list could be more extensive, but what I found intriguing were the translations—how sexist the language was, the fear of the feminine, how domestic, how patriarchal, how imaginative, and the beauty I discovered when I paused to wonder about the humanity inside these words and phrases. I realized that the labels we use to name present us with a loss. To name a person, an experience, or an object means we see it for that purpose, that utility, and gone to us is the "what else"—the possibilities of everything that the label can't encompass. I wanted the poems in this collection to uncover the unseen, to find and engage a connection that allowed me to make meaning of my own, and to pulse with a rhythm that could more accurately re-sound life, not just identity and its embedded disconnections. These terms, from which a majority of the poems take their titles, became a way of residing in the body, inviting the charge of the words, accounting for my response, and witnessing—the mundane, the quotidian, violence, social divides, emotions like grief and love—through a queer lens. Which is to say, seeing everything as its own passing presence.

Tail

There are little words
that can fit in little places
if you say them small enough.

To fit a song into a pore
you have to be prepared
for the day it will sweat.

If words could stick to people,
they would become different
creatures when spoken.

Blindfolded and turned
five times around, nothing
in you knows what it knew.

This is the fun part:
Prick the girls you like best
while pinning the donkey's tail.

Six Colors

Sounds the body
makes to keep quiet
while I take
your camisole down:
purple. Our sable bodies
an inappropriate math
in one stall.

From the time you fell
in a puddle
in Fort Greene Park,
I keep taking
off your socks,
faded red,
keep flagging
them on a stick,
in the sun. Love,
as third graders,
we knew.

After school,
hard like unripe,
the handball
rubbed off its blue.
Hands on hips,
arms like chevrons,
you served attitude.
Legs as long
as the parkway,
your bra strap
slipped, and now
slips, pink.

With Feathers

She runs the girl to her knees after a chase around the temple, wades through a moat of oversized clothes to find secrets the girl cares for like children: the dream:

> She looks warrior-some, striking the air, can fall like a feather. She is solar and soaring, and it's nice to avoid the shade when she's out. There's something I can map out in her: home—the spades and bones slapped on fold-out tables, old women with hot-comb scars and the iron's triangle; pyramids of fallen roofs, beneath the rubble the spell that cast a neighbor's tongue carp; the chipped ceramic bowl that crushed the leaves to take the devil's heat gone. Never before would I think the cartographer needed to put handles on maps but she needs a strong invitation to be held.

I wake and bring myself back from the Icarian tattoo on your arm:

> In sleep her words are her own. They are in the shape of her Halmonie pass, petite and hunched, watching the pinched ways we lie to the heart. She couldn't bury her talk if she wanted to. Halmonie: the one who molded her sounds into proper ornaments.

> That wing's a slow-etch of a species her skeleton can't support. She remains pedestrian, saddened by an immigrant tale of too many hushes, an army base, a war that brought soldiers and converted women to pastime reds.

> She is pretty and perfect in sleep before language must be assigned— she knows too little of one, much of the other, and the rest of the time being human leads us to scan the hem of an island with our sweat for show.

I walk into the morning's fog, its intimate silence. I'm a single letter rescued from the caul of sleep. These are my mouths, this murder of black hands in grace over harvested earth:

> *Amen to the fields that grow corn, pumpkin, squash, and*
> *potatoes. The dirt is the start for dinner. Did the farmer find*
> *my panty and her house keys, or was a crop nurtured by our*
> *scent, the secrets we parse to each other, the debris, hauled*
> *and abandoned because of a look? Eat, for better the journey,*
> *for better the love. I carry less sin and more sky that says,*
> *This when to plant, this when to let her rest.*

Their hunger commits them to the ground. The crow from
your back woke this morning to revel in the company of
common plumage, to break the confines of your skin, to caw at
my approach, and with a look, invites my stare into something
without cage or collar:

> *This is how lovers look at each other when they have seen*
> *beneath the clothes. When daytime is not the time to know.*
> *We still want, and the silence we consent to makes grief in*
> *our smiles. We cover our eyes like mirrors and our mouths*
> *take the blandest of meals. We starve the desire that fattens*
> *the heart, that requires space and reach we're afraid to give—*
> *it sets a fleet of monarchs from our chests; we try to catch and*
> *are left dusted.*

Paw

One of a million women on many buses to Pennsylvania,
I'm new meat. She's a college senior. Alpha-stagger
assesses if this is a piece to be tossed or left—
if I can last the short-fast road between her paws.

She sets back the pack, brushes her curls
from her eyes. I believe my childhood cat
taught me how to receive her, how to welcome
after the previous smiles have failed.

I cannot take on her sorrow's torch,
it withers bright beneath a roofless stare—
she wants me to stay.

My eyes travel Philly's curbs,
enter the rust and tongueless Liberty Bell,
loop then double-constrict her wrists,
and we agree—*bananas* for safety.

Who Invited the Monkey To Omen's Party?

Easthampton, Massachusetts

You are enamored with the tall man with a fountain of dreadlocks. You take Lucas's invite to come to Chrissie's. She is a pixie plucked of her wings and missing a wand, tells you she painted your portrait without knowing you. We take your friend's Saturn down a circuitous route, rain-slick as a seal, back to her place. Omen answers the ring in his pocket. His words are slippery. He chills the nape of your neck with a dewy happy birthday song. Maggie drives the car. If she were naked she would be Botticelli's half-shelled lady. We arrive after many left turns. Lucas pisses in the parking lot. You watch the dirt steam the isosceles of his legs. You help Omen up the stairs. His left cheek blushes a keloid crescent. You come to an apartment painted mango inside. A Doberman sniffs your patella, and then whips you with his tail; your scent is of no use. In the bedroom, Bob Marley reggaes low. Chrissie shows you your face, charcoal and sleeping in an atmosphere of green. The dreadlocked man tells you his name is Kevin; his voice lacks the volume of his hair. He passes you the bong; you've forgotten how. Cough and swallow your spit to extinguish the burning. You exhale, sit back, and watch Omen balance a lighter on your shoe. You offer him water for his vertigo. Alexis arrives with dilated pupils. Omen plays the djembe with his forehead. Then foot. Alexis mumbles, *Who invited the monkey to Omen's party?* You look at her for clarification. Porcelain-doll eyes don't meet yours. You or Omen? You, they just met in the bar. You, the only one in the room who looks like you, besides the poster of Buju Banton and the oil painting of the woman that reminds you of the West Indian lady who sells Avon products on Utica Ave back in Brooklyn. Maggie heard too and shares your blinking confusion. You both fib, *It was nice meeting everyone.* She drives you home. Turns up her protestations and lowers the radio. She steers herself through the fissures that synapsed this occurrence. You smoke a mint Nat Sherman. It's midnight past thirty and the first time you've ever turned simian.

Auntie

I listen for you in these moments of touch,
declare through your friends what is not said.

                    I inventory looks, languishing on the sweet end
          of a woman's backside, her body, their eyes silk over
               air we just breathed, blink and their lids rest
             like water to shore, relishing as one does a kiss.

This orchestrated silence is viral; it heats
all parts until my throat fevers.
How do you manage this, auntie?

            When your friends are around, your hands language
               near her to confirm she's close: on her forearm,
                  the small of her back, you hold often,
              fingering notes to release perfect sound.

Together since the year of my birth,
yet you are pantomime in the wings
of our family's speech.

                  Why do you arch in shadows,
             accept the shade eclipsing her face?

The holidays would be more gay
if we didn't ghost in dead air,

in wooden boxes,   letters folded over and over again,   in locked rooms

               where shames are secretly arranged—

Drag Up

*dedicated to the white people who were asked to raise their
hands if they would choose to be black*

Every month she buys magazines of haute couture,
takes them home to Washington Heights,
and clips out models. *It is not their color,*
my 22-year-old girlfriend contests, *it's how well
their bodies display clothes.* A point, she makes it
to tell me about this white woman's nose, she likes
this white woman's lips, another's eyes, white
cheekbones she saves in piles on the floor, in files
on the bookshelf, these faces, from their bodies,
snapshot and stored beneath her bed.

A trunk, she pulls out, of three hundred Barbie dolls.
Takes the lid off a collection, white and naked, jostles
like sugar cane cut foot-long, stretched out side by side,
each head at the feet of her neighbor, face up, smiling.
All these plastic bodies have names: Sarah, Cora, Theresa,
Jane. . . . To my face, she puts two, close, pale and thin,
smells like condensed milk—*The hairline,* she says,
is what makes them really distinct.

She tells me how they came into her possession.
In plastic containers she places their accessories,
of the time when she saw them on the shelf.
She explains how she makes their outfits. She always
buys another when she passes a toy store—
between breasts and thighs her fingers go.
Wipes their lips, a new color she branded, the browner
version of eyebrows to their forehead. She arranges
her dolls back in rows, piles on Barbie piles, no space is wasted.
Twist-ties their wrists and legs, so when she puts on the cover,
they won't kick and their hands won't raise.

Inconvenient Roof

If your dog died, you would love me more,
although I'm frightened the roof will cave in
if the dog is removed from the triangle.

Cards lean to form a satisfying equilateral.
I didn't consider diamond and club as sheetrock
on a pocket of air, or balance as conversation

until the thing the other covets is gone. How much
I can hold, how much you can—the forecast changes.
I'm left with your disconsolate sails,

your body sinking to old-womb comforts—
a grown sorrow to suckle, my breasts can't pretend.
I don't know what to do with vacuums—

my hands aren't spades for that kind of earth.
My mother tended her own plots.
Carved out the yard and buried cutouts of him.

She was the fence. I beware not to fall
into a pocket of grief, kept my arms
to the sides—breaking her I couldn't afford.

If she could swallow herself she would.
I had to reverse my wish. *Come back
to me, the snow's falling.*

Left

When I first saw it, the birthmark,
a strip of dried papaya on your cheek,
I thought, *Your mother craved Cuba.*

It's not Spanish that comes out—
your Brooklyn-born self
knows how to ask "How are you?"
but you don't respond to the question.

Your voice, shorelines and the city.
In your throat you carry
the weight of cleansed land

and dirty words that leave
you feeling like you can lick
the side of a building and kiss
the prettiest girl on the block.

We laugh as off-keys clink
against tiles, fall into the bath,
and cling to our toes for rescue.

Good notes we keep for ourselves.
My listening ear tossed from a body
gone wrinkled from soaking,
a bouquet you catch with winks.

You say, *Baby, this one's for you.*
Strum guitar from your navel,
lick the mole of sweat from your lip—

the song brewing for at least a decade
in your belly's cellar, waiting
for this day, this splash,
the light to invite it out.

Strangers

Dark as an illegal,
may beetles fall on us and the closed gas station.
Once a water bug hung from my headscarf.
It was the touch of someone coming from behind.
We're lost in Texas. Hit a dead deer and there goes
the wheel off our trailer. Sorry you left your camp gear
on the roadside. I forgot to say thank you, I was afraid.
We're queer and you look too much boy and good thinking
taking the rainbow off the plates in Maryland—
no one looked at us longer than needed.

Now we're at the point where we can't wake
ourselves up. We didn't start out on back roads—
on Route 9, in a college town, I whispered,
I want to hang from her wallet chain.
You heard, stopped at the path's end.
I approached but this dark is not your smile.
Your chain is noise in a Texan's sleep. You step
into the light to pick up a signal, the least distracted
by beetles, and the wish being made on us tonight.

Dagger

My freedom was learned twice by fire.
My lover's stove took over, every hair brought to ash.
I was later told, *Good thing you didn't breathe,*
the flame would have found energy for more.

The hellfire was not what my brother described.
I dropped chocolate from my s'mores onto the charcoals
and nobody cried. He said I would be punished, be party
to the woman who proved her devotion by eating her lover's
endometrial waste—*is this what you want to do as a lesbian?*

His thoughts are poor, simple in geometric shape. Fits dogma
in his mouth like woof and barks a testament he can't substantiate.
It's choice. He beats Qur'an instead of his necrotic heart. Murder is not
the point of my life—left to live in cells of his correction, in least
populated hours, dismissed of my caw—

We fly branch-tethered. They know their heirlooms' cost,
woven to make suffering tight, their heads can't turn, fearing
a salt-pillar's life. We need to let angels in our doors, every creature
needs stranger company to know the nay and yea of its comportment,
the topography and unmentionables of its god.

Surprised I've become the self I consented to—
maybe now they'll see the river plainly in their faces,
their smiles without flood, silt-rich and begging. Here,

my seed as natural as the sheath you put me in.

Lilla, Inscribed

Bluebells, poppies, Jack-in-the-pulpit, columbines, Queen Anne's lace,
blazing stars, and Georgia O'Keefe was an impeccable florist. You'd
think the canvas was the flower and only this flower, and your world
was this flower, close and intimate, this flower you could put your hand
inside a blush, and bless yourself after you've sneezed. Lilly—the first
time God blessed me. She was in my painting class for beginners. She
knew the steps for getting the canvas ready. I needed words for my latest
strokes, needed to place letters on her lips. She invited my mouth and let
my Pilot turn her body to written—to free verse from our frictions, our
make-believes, our sighed-through fists.

Her cosmos navel Her moss plexus Her skin

Your letter a garden to turn, even the
kitchen courts birds of paradise. It's the
sun on the curtains and they say you
should begin your morning with shine—
and so the first directive of my day: rise.
Will you wake up with me?

Her daisy breast Her glory tit Her clavicle

I know you, I feel you when distance
puts borders and tunnels between us,
spineless roads. Across a track, on a city's
nerves—let us not be the last. Say you
love me not? It's true, my thing for you
takes rules away. Now the clouds have
clocks.

Her standing thigh Her sweet peduncle Her legs

Meet me at an hour on a day that'll
forever repeat. On Tuesdays I need my
watering. I have been wonderful in
fragments, tail-less with blindfolded luck,
but how long will that last? Pennies can't
keep flowers forever and regret won't.

Her hands Her hands Her hands

I don't look lost with you in front. You
are key. Come inside, I'll nuke the tea. I
fix what's wrong and spend struggles.
The history books should include more
romance, when girls rubbed the feet of
their friends after boycotts, wiped spit
from cheeks, blood from chins.

Her iliac crest Her four-dot blades Her tidy neck

We can get back to start and win again;
it's a matter of changing where the race
begins. Fire in the night is not always a
reason to run; it's a reason to make sure
what's important to us is protected. Do
you prefer bright or neutral colors on the
walls?

Her scarlet tongue Her rolling brow Her wild lashes

The portrait and the reflection don't
match but soon enough we will catch up
to that face. The stereo is loud and we are
abominable's spawn—thankfully our
mothers cannot eat us. Paper has its
margins, the boulevard has its curbs; I'm
right outside and between cocoons.

Her feet Her Nyabinghi soles Her toes Her toes Her toes

The body shows its persistence against
insult and sticks and I am not afraid:
come for my wallet, put me in debt, bully
my wit to stubborn.

Her flipped bird Her bar-back biceps Her no-Adam rib

Endearments are the finest threads that
keep the skin from apart. It has taken me
years to find the right one: *Swiss, Sugar
Blossom, Le Muff* never stays where it's
put, doesn't keep pattern, unravels the
warm.

Her trapezius Her candy 'lobes Her armpits

The promise seals us and I promise to
not put you in a box, promise to polish
the stones that keep the blade from
reaching our hearts, promise to replace
sips with half gallons, promise to wash
forks, promise to deliver this into the
postman's hands.

Her body Her body Her body

Sometimes in people there are crumbs
that lead to a prouder welcome. . . .
Here, my fear to love builds a wall, a
bridge, and should I Berlin or Benedict?

Torn

Can hold a whole block inside of me—
intersections, streetlights. The Lakeshore
Bar with boomers Chicago stepping. The lake
between, the hill that demands a lion's share
of breath, and I'm climbing it.

There is a woman ripping sheets of paper
into small tablets. Holds them until her
hands fill and precipitate. Sections read:
can't be with— and *need to*—. She sobs
one paper-cut width at a time.

I hear my letters opening, why this is
not working. Never on the other side
of the envelope, sealed with a kiss she will
tear through. Part sigh and panic, mail is
better at saying these things.

My heart is not brave in confrontation,
it can easily return to a relationship that needs
trees and bushes to keep it from slipping—
I'm not ready to plant. I avoid certain streets
to avoid women who stay with me like sand.

Gun(n)

for Sakia Gunn

Sakia, if you had the weapon of your last name,
I would not know you. This steady scrape
against paper to transport fecund lament, never.
If in your hands the pearl-handled gun

my stepfather kept in the broom closet—
I'd give you the aim I practiced at twelve.
"Home is where the heart is" marks an
average man's forehead and the trashcan
is somewhere near his jewels.

If you brought me roses in high school,
wrapped in newspaper to protect me from thorns,
I would take them, and wash ink from my fingers
in the jeans and jersey flood of your girlboy body.
Let me be your girl.

4-evah 2 eternity onto my back.
Your finger's ballpoint end, again and again
practices the heart over *i*, and into the morning
we stash whispers where over thread, thread crosses.
I promise

I have impeccable aim.
Pulling a trigger loosens mustangs
in your veins. Piss into my mortar—an old war
recipe makes bullets complete. Let your shower
wash an asshole from the streets.

If blood quickly betrays its avenues
for Newark's sidewalks, his shirt tires of its thirst. . .
If his buddy drives him to the hospital
or leaves him to watch the night unspool—
what a Jacob's Ladder he makes . . .

If you're shocked your life requires this exchange,
come into my arms, Sakia. Come into my arms.

Trip the Light Fantastic

I'm the lady in the joint without a G-string and Brazilian chocha.
Winter-dressed and the money in my pocket affords me a Heineken.
I have no ones to offer thighs that can headlock Washington.
Coins work best for parking meters and fountains.

When the next dancer arrives to stage, she wipes the pole
with a moist napkin—the abracadabra is gone.
Gestures to the wall to press start, positions her blanket
so it doesn't abandon her when she werks her alphabet.

She takes an interest in me—this is not ego—
sees the wardrobe of long sleeves and pants in how I stare.
Weeks ago, I saw her forefinger in some butch's belt loop;
coupled like his and hers towels. Maybe she noticed me then.

She comes to my earring and requests, *Slap my ass.*
Shakes it like wind went through her leaves.
My hands on pause. She laughs
then brings her undulations to a man in woodsman flannel.

She returns her legs, fans the sweet of green
apples ripe in my nose. In doggy style, demonstrates.
Her spank is the thud of unbreakable dishware.
Again—whoa!—No shatter.

She encourages me, recognizes this is my first time on a two-wheeler.
The Heineken cools the singing in my palm. I'm ordered
to give it to her, and like the kid in band who plays
cymbals, counting to cue, I make her bottom ring like Saturn.

Blue Boy

Blue boy, blue boy, blue blue boy. Is it possible something that royal stepped outside of me? Boy: spent the morning painting himself, his lashes hold original color. Blue that deserves a stick stuck into it and shade to delay sugar from going down your hand. And is it possible that a body can borrow a wave and move tides high? Move moon? Move seasons to wine? I follow him down Eastern Parkway through a crowd flagged in island colors, watch his hips bat wind 'round. He bumps against me, streaks my forearm. His sweat is there too. His teeth, white-white. *Ya gonna take off me make-up before a gal can get through de parade.* Girl: I heard like it was the oldest and newest.

Bat

All that time you spend in the mirror
you're best to gauge attractiveness, how
an eye is to suggest alertness, innocence,
coquettish come-come—all the more to bella
donna your frightened arched kitties.
Are we to judge the lives *you've* lived?
If not for hide to hold skeletons, your ugly
would be eating the floor. Some of us
carry it to show or to tell and listening closely,
you see it. The concave part where you're missing
love resonates back its garlic-fart nectar,
and you wonder how I could kiss *her*.

Whole Lot of Lot

Assed out, my withered ego hydrates on English Breakfast.

I loved a girl who ashed her cigarette into days-old Lipton
        and the mug grew a universe with particular dysfunctions:

           The ladies, if there were ladies,
           kept letting their hair down for rescue—
           each tug and pull affirmed she was loved

           Some noble savages got distracted by lint
           and parasites and spent generations
           picking and nibbling, they never faced her

The sea has a way of bringing us to our depths

Immaculate birth is a challenge to life yourself—imagine:
        linked to your navel a newer you,
           calls and calls, (connect, connect, connect),
                drags you along like a Texan Byrd

feet lose communication with head—separation breeds brutal action—
        cells dispersed on backs of bees
           you reshape and forest

        We always hear when we fall

                Trust me

           It's an alarm to arms:

           stretch out, bare skin,

        the sun will defend you, and in this state,

        don't settle for the first pants that find you.

Warm Water

The narrative that I do not belong is in the spindle of my spine, in a biorhythm part Nae Nae and Wop, as a translation generations removed from meaning—these are my crying thirties.

Where I'm caught, between past and ASAP, you are the representative of all who could not risk an act of love. Waking the dream is hard. Hard to object you. Hard to know there is no more than what, here, is.

I'm fatigued by the going. People say, *You are young, you don't crack.* And they laugh a murder. I read them, they read me, they stare. I cry privately. My sorrow means they've found amending.

We are in clouds, on ice and horses and smoking our way to the morning's edge. We sip life neat. Medicate so not to feel the root. I go there, too, to sulk, to touch again what you deny. Key "Coward" on the driver's side, "Cunt" for anyone who takes passage with you.

For the consequences of my desire, I cry. For those times in my youth when I was free and unaware and could turn a woman into a monsoon. Could strip my skin, step inside out, leave my bones for looking.

We give up so much not to be seen. In all these "nevers" and "I won't," I made a home in places where I didn't. There is no one familiar here. Not you to love me, not a one.

Make a body out of my sobs and the greenest grass grows. In the cemetery, the tombs were petrified by their loneliness. Bring me deep blues, bring me to my violets.

I bring up femurs and think in triangles, and I'm holy. I am canyon and echo of curious voices, aren't you moved? Their chatter, cherry blossoms and hail; their longing, cicadas.

Hoping it will come back to welcome, I drag our placenta behind me. Together can be restored with a blink. My thread, where are you? I have no more needles to spare.

I am at your doorstep. Each tear opens us up to our promise—bring the wake of your hand to my cheek. What I need today is your sunshine that pulls me from earth.

Dirty Fruit

She holds herself out to me,
a portion she knows I'm willing to eat.
Bows her head over her legs—I'm here
to be reminded of ifs, tea was an excuse.
She confesses she slept with my ex—once,
holds a finger up to let me count
her solemn swear.

Does the priest ever beat the confessor
until his disgust stampedes her face,
until spit is violent, until I've spent
all there is to spend cracking her chest?

—my heart can't eat from this orchard.

Passing

The cross on his chest made my body the barer. Compelled
to be a blanket, fur; however he would have me, he had me.
His god was something to hang on to. A chain that made
return possible. My reflection sullied the gold.

The house we couldn't build across from the house I wouldn't

Miracles happen across from when whiskey happens, across

from the magenta room that couldn't—Oaksterdam couldn't

Hotel California across from *Broaster's Chicken Coming Soon*

Men, when they do, cross their legs in the way of academics.
Never in the way of churchwomen who keep the secret
covered—there's nothing to be implored, explored, discovered.
In the way of academics, the whole body thinks. To the side,
he shows a chin propped by a fist, between his cheeks
thought is candy, eyes turn skyward. In the way of
churchwomen their eyes look down, to their breast,
beneath their shirt, to the source of much anxiety, a nipple,
pleasured by Pastor Rayon's touch.

City Line is a hand hennaed and scarred

Retro lift the Victorian's scaffolded west

Free Baby Jamaica from the bus's accordion folds

Black & White the street for a frantic Dodge, a passenger lost

I cross my t's and men are dying. The bushes sing baritone
and contralto, from someone's gut a baby's born. For every

shattered stair, men are folding into each other, bodies pressed and puzzled. There's comfort knowing his edge has a home. In a cup or covering the chest, he values sunrise, for days to speed, for the soul to let go bone. He the more aware death's a trespasser, and the heart will bark till red meat turns it elsewhere—a man at the end of wait.

Rent-a-Relic says no to Proposition 8

Rainbows bend on International Boulevard, wilted and prostituted

Pirates who negotiate with raccoons concubine and divide The Merritt

Senior citizens weep willows in Ogawa and native yards

Cross my heart and hope, a needle in the eye. The cross is an X, really. Is how to find a treasure. How to hug at the end of a letter. If you dig where I mark, what do you do with the gravel, the flesh that slips back into the hole? Mail it to my brother; he's the most poetic. He'll oil it with colors, attend verse after verse with the breathiest weather, a text you can prism.

Comrades

1. there is a father

In the usual fog evening, San Francisco at eight,
the second whiskey served—and generous pours—
four pulls from my girl's homegrown sativa, and I was mingling
before, but the edge has been smoothed, so I mingle more.

     A few moments ago, before the sun had an official set,
your wife said she blew her whole wad driving east to west.
I couldn't help but hoot, joked I would be spent by Philly.

     It's good when the entire group laughs, and you turn
the conversation to Mormons—in Salt Lake you can't *ask*
for doubles. Your wife says, *Gotta learn the lingo to get what you want.*

     And think in a place where you can have
two wives but not two shots, you say. I look skyward,
think hoodoos and driving a stick into mountains,

     Even then, the second one you don't ask for!
You laugh me into loving you. My heart, radiant in my chest,
opens evenly to grief: where has my father gone? Luckily, I'm a dead-on
for my mother, I knew I belonged.

     You shout, *Tell it again.* Call the crowd to my attention—
Tell it again and I'm too shy to remember the last time I saw
him, arms outstretched, kneeling: we were the same height. Strange
the delight this stranger had for me. My mother said, *That is your father*—
I hid behind a door and saw the blue my girl beautifies.

     On the drive back home, I smile. I heard you smile too,
trying the timing and wording of my wit.

2. there is a missing number 9

Twelve years of no dental insurance and 60 percent
of bone loss later, I don't have a front tooth and it's
Martin Luther King, Jr. Day in 2004. We pay
for one movie, sneak into two, and while cars race

furious on the screen and the popcorn is down
to a pop, you show me a gala.

The flipper will flip out like the time a Dorito dislodged
it and to the concrete it fell and a pair of Dominican nannies
watched me slip it back into my mouth, and so you understand—
when I point to my teeth—the troubles apples get women into
and your bite is strong.

Separation of apple piece from apple whole
is heart warming and you hand me a chunk, then one
for yourself, you chew and chew, then bite off another
and between the race on the screen we get to the core
and I say, *Enjoy.*

3. *there is an island*

You drive and drive and the land looks the same.
Two hours back, they called it something.
Two hours forward, they'll call it different.
Intending to toss the pear's core, you call for me to stop.

Places not city look the same to me.
You nod and say, *This is the best part.*
Islanders move at the pace of growing breast—
you bite, between your teeth the fruit's umbilical line.

You drive everywhere and wherever there's rain,
the smell: washed rice, turtle shells, cucumbers sliced.
You put the remainder of core in my mouth.
The seeds on my tongue make a reptilian face.

You pull over, and we're barefooted
in the flooded part of the road. I run
a barrel amount of crabs to scuttle. You watch

me discover what now doesn't get wasted.

4. *there is a station wagon*

My pager beeps in the night's middle. You want to drive
to the Lower East Side and drink wine until wine drinks us.

A cheese plate joins our glasses and the next idea we'll roost
in our hearts, and this is what I love most about your heart.

Full of light and everglade. You traveled to the bayou
for weeks to drum and dance, brought me back a sarong,

colored menses and Indian gold. You tell me, *I wasn't
going to get you nothing but my mind changed.*

A fresh feeling for outside brunching, we plan our hunger
two days from now. And you will pick me up in this station wagon

from your twenties—five holes in its back panel. *Oshun's number,*
you say, as we Manhattan Bridge into the break of dawn.

5. *there is a scotch bonnet*

The tongue is a patchwork quilt.
Land is feet squared at altitudes
from New York to Cancun—
a part sweet, sour,
a part bitter, salty.

I tell him candy, my toddler
brother opens his mouth.
Who is he to question

these hands that said,
Come, come on first steps?

The scotch bonnet burns.
I float in the princess cut of his tears,
counting cornrows before the plane
leaves behind a soot-stamp earth.

Indifferent to how wind blows,
to the degrees it takes to reach bone,
I smell caramelized sugar in a boy's hair.

I return to him with laughter,
sliced bread—he rejects,
wipes his mouth like a squeegee
can get it back to clean.

To be forgiven, his body must be persuaded.
The fruit roll-up I offer as remedy.
I wait: this time the green
is apple and sweet.

6. *there is steaming bergamot*

You

tell me to enjoy the tea without sugar—simple as coming inside
and taking off my shoes. Doing so keeps the carpet clean, the street
closer to the door—but since I knew tea only with sugar, it's the
beginning of my subtraction lesson.

                              You hold my hand
to cross Amsterdam, to St. John the Divine. I forget the feeling of

adult care, because, on her own, a big girl can get to the other side. I moved too slow for you. *Use them legs, girl.* I stretched them long.

You're the second one

I've lost to AIDS. I'm a freshman in my dorm, and I pray. In the early morning, your cologne opens my eyes and brings to the window two deer on the arm of a fallen tree.

7. there is a Huffy

I learned to ride on the sweet
cojones of my gumption.
No one ever taught me.

My friend thought he was
cute, I liked his Huffy,
and asked like I knew.

Around the block twice,
I went by with ease,
biked through a building,

a fence—came out diamond-
shaped and committed
my black fist to the air.

A two-by-four to soar over milk
crates, and a mattress-safe landing
held my gratitude: thank you,
small and necessary step.

Little Deer

She drinks in passers go by, sings Vandross,
lets me linger between blinks with no odor that I am here.

I'm tempted to give up on sound to labor.
I can't go wrong—she's a prize of her species.

Pull up my sleeves, grab the boombox and stand without outlet,
disappear before her curtains part—she felt my ten-speed jet.

Her whole body lightning awesome;
beneath her laughter shimmers a bolt.

Her birthmark traveled since her birth,
now stationed over heart, and we have the same cuba.

I'm giddy—forgot to answer her question with my name.
She will forget my portrait in these museums.

We miss seeing full circle by 50 degrees.
I step outside her blind spots, and summer there.

Hold still, I tell my feet, please meet noon
even as thirsty and irritable virgins.

I'm lured by my nature, persistent as a root. To enter
home range without a gift in hand is as rude as weeds.

Willing to share all that is extra beneath my flesh:
bone, platelets, eggs or whatever she craves.

There is something silk and right about her—
water generous and hair good to breathe.

Chance Is Based On True Events

Walk down the street, everybody
knows your need to touch her.
Smile a smile in a smile,
and feel that kind of marathon.

Swing on that spine
between your birth days
until sleep wants you.

Have the body
with its flames
and charities
and its rooms to cry

Until the war is out
of its actors and casualties,
be grizzly on the floor.

Look up—
rarely do we look up.
There are kisses and hugs
above us—kisses and hugs.

Swear on old and new
that the wind shakes
the picture admired too long.

Take a chance,
be houndish and address
her in stranger shapes.

Love her to the crunch,
to a barbaric end
with song and spittle,
pinball and bric-a-brac.

Hold Your Part of a Deal

To know something singular in yourself is amazing, nothing gets in the way. No sentence forever failing because it can't match. It is painful truth with a runner's pulse, a touch that's down and there you are with a woman-all-legs.

You say yes to her after the initial hello—she speaks and the want is forever need. You in her kitchen with a third, fourth glass, finding something opening. There is fever, rage that you've been closed, and now you're coming back to life after being asleep on it.

(Everything is in a hurry, in retreat—this will not last long. The habit requires you to flee before she reaches, take bits of the self you can carry. You marched, you marched and oh, you marched. She sees you running and grabs your hand, tells you, *Put it down; let it go.* You become possessive.)

You're thirsty and any old tap won't do. It becomes a joke about how you U-Haul. You and her till dying, and when seasons come and go, days link to scents, her cycles, and you learn no tomatoes, extra mayo, always on white. You fall asleep breathing together—you know when balance has changed, notice different chimes in her laugh, the late-night draft through your window, soon you get cold. She's not caring she's taking too much cover.

All you know of yourself is that tick, measuring the length of her absence. What you take, no more, because what you built was not known to shake and crumble, divide halfway without you knowing who's getting your half.

Sips turn into confidence, you need to ask. She is holy in her lies and the grapevine frequents your shoulder to say, *You're being treated a fool.*

(What is the point to opening and opening you betray the home inside of you? Expose its rooms and its clutter, dust, the child with your face, peeling at her lips to get to the tender part of a kiss. Opening the wind so it leaves its sand and salt to glitter scars, until you see there are pearls to give you worth—opening and opening to abandon even yourself?)

You are in prairies of hurt, bold and cageless, when bullets make a space for two more stars, and a headline of how you took her first then followed.

Effluvium

for Karen, 1963—2000

My Dead

Everybody she died another is dead everybody
dead and AIDS of AIDS my dead she is
there are more I know with the same story hiding
lips stitched hesitant to speak of someone you knew
how we cast dirt on the dead long before they've reached
how we shun those who don't die natural
who lose themselves in dissolution
we give them our backs
our unguarded susurrations: she should   she should
she should've known better
sleeping with some shiftless recovering drug addict
she should   she should she she she is my dead
clicking dying bones on the periphery
we could no longer match the beauty we knew
genital warts the size of her son's two-year-old fists
she had them laser removed
it hurt to walk it hurt so bad to take a piss
so bad ached her thighs who would love her then

with my hands I would step her from her clothes
undress myself and sit legs parted waiting
to fit her behind in the curve of pelvic bone
I part and grease her scalp love her hair into cornrows
against the cliffs of her shoulder blades then we are people
we meet down South we got genealogy we are familiar
she is my dead in my arms on my collar her head rests
her breasts capitulate her body's a summer hymn I breathe
she opens to my half prayer moans her architecture burst

an alchemy of sea and sun   and she   and she

        and she   and spice   and she

                and sugar   she   and love

                and she   and she
and nice

                and she's my dead—

                        water in my hands

[]
The first thing my mother says when I get off the plane from Ghana, *You have to see Karen.* I say, *I will.* I say, *I will.* I went off to the Berkshires, in the mountains, to administer to dancers and didn't go. To what would have been the final time I would see you. Four weeks later, you died. I didn't go. I didn't take a bus to your funeral. I didn't borrow the money. I didn't ask. Anyone would have.

This Place

Where you are, is it a ventricle in the sky
that night when clouds arranged themselves
a spine across a deeper navy?

are you placed in the meeting of bones and discord?
the other day I found my knees grinding, was that you
frustrated with not being heard, you came in arthritic code?
some pretend your absence has taken you from our touch,
but they hold you between the pause and pulse.

this place where you are is it in the mourning of your son?
Granny still has the newspaper clipping. your mother said
he looked like he was asleep, after falling six stories. lashes
lined with the cracks, feet planted in the dirt where flowers
grow your favorite color. it is the rose your first-born loves.
your name is tattooed on the opposite side of her throat.
you will see her calling without being witness to her mouth.

I could be placed where you are. so hard what makes this—
fear to ask anyone about you. to wash this quiet. questions
break them. they stomach their shards. talk with mangled
mouths. things already heard come from them. we stand
before sorrow, cousin. our clauses don't travel. we've
imagined collisions. we faint. our arms wither when trying
to hold this: your dead self, how do we love?

When They Say

you are pretty, they come with pretty things to match you. believe
them like you are the fourteen year old who's taken into an alley,
gasoline poured in your honor, you are drenched in flames

Was I black and ugly?

pretty are you to officials who order your dissident pink
extinct of eagles. just and blind in their examination, they flip
the switch to make you forget yourself celestial and rising

Was I crazy in love?

you are the drug, the pretty to the schizophrenic who snorts
coke off your pubic bone, takes a swig of Cola, and his friends
watch him insert vacuum attachments into your snatch

Why did he do that to me?

pretty girl you are whose uncle comes for a visit and molests
you at the dinner table. you are the pretty mother loving
you years later who says, *We all must go through it*

Why is this what they leave for me?

so young and pretty, so tight you are virgin mythologized.
left broken to cup the spilling of a positive penis, from your
edges come no cure, your adolescence initiated with AIDS

Who would touch me like this?

pretty clit clipped and sewn, military shotgun shattered
vaginal walls, your people cannot stand the smell of your shards.
you are bruised pretty to miscarry an undesirable girl

Why am I here?

you are the gash who never stops bleeding, whose ovaries
scream and eggs drop as they please, your uterus diagnosed
hysterical. you are without the possibility of gardens

Am I?

Karen, you are holy ova, she-she serenade, potent dap and dynahara,
bornship and portal, worshipped lotus, you are liminal wonder,
helicun, you are vivakiss, kush, fragrant red-deep, a woke-parade—
believe, you are the most beautiful thing that happened.

[]

You are frozen by a camera's lens, smiling. There is one with you holding me and I'm dressed in a sailor suit. This is how I remember you now. The last time you came around you were wearing a wig. Your skin, a tight and shiny brown found on fake things. You were in white. If I hugged you, I don't know. My eyes held you from a distance, blinking out: Where have you been? Why you look like that? How are you? Then, I did not know. You grinned at all the faces that grinned. I know I said hello. I must have.

Introduction

She is my cousin who found out she was infected when she gave birth to her second child. he died at two. they are all my cousins. she is my first. I drag her everywhere. her funeral wear is ragged. I exhume her each night to apologize, beg her for her story, and she tells me she has nothing more to say. she says she has lost her words in the dirt and needs to find them. meet her, maybe she will tell you something she has not told me. maybe she will read beneath your skin and tell me you are safe and I will not die opening my legs to you. stand up, she must bless you. come from under the covers. show yourself. turn around. stretch out your arms: he is long. he is beautiful. his ass is pleasure. his feet without callouses. nothing stains his hands. turn around. his teeth are straight. he is cake, cousin. Guard our coitus with your effluvium and Death will think we've been marked.

[]

I still haven't visited your grave. I am afraid to see people wilt before tombstones, whole bodies weeping, remembering what the dead ones left behind. And the silence of the cemetery swallows this all, people appear as pantomimes of mourning. I don't want to talk to you in the open. The wind is a thief. The dirt takes everything and buries it. For three years you've been six-feet deep. I've savored this sorry as if it were the sweet in Hojo's mouth.

I would begin by wiping my lips at your plot, the way you did after you kissed Hojo in the elevator of your mother's apartment building. You and him stood in the smell of urine and liquor, eyes meeting eyes, and I looked up to your profiles. You sucking on hard candy, he asked for some. You brought your kiss to his, your tongue rolled the cherry bomb behind his teeth, and I thought that was the perfect way to share.

Kokobar

I. *Good Mornings*

People stand reading muffins, careful
cursive of daily specials, peering
through bagels, for hunger has made them
strangely curious as I watching
through lashes the woman with eyes
the color of concrete before it settles.

She smiles and ponytails her dreadlocks.
To say more than good morning
sounds the danger of loose shoestrings—
a scraped conversation to impede
the unbuttoning that might bring her closer.

And like any dutiful customer,
I give her my order and hope she grabs
the roasted beans with naked hands.

II. *Cyber lounge*

The computers to my profile, the books steep
in green tea walls, her head mostly afro,
her dress fans the floor. She
taps the keys with one hand.

The other day, I walked to her,
asked about what she's reading.
She pearls her speech with "Smoke, Lilies, Jade,"
turns the book over, its spine furrows:

Black girls… talking… about fucking… girls.
Seasons changed in my cheeks,
I couldn't excuse my petals.

Blinking offered minute
darkness to hide and paw
my way to the door.

Today, I make her not notice me.
Brooklyn watches through the window,
a perfect screen for my staring heart.

III. *Oh,*

I was teenaged, searching for a face
to reflect my own who would call me beautiful
enough to make me think it's possible she's not lying.

The day and night dream had its floors littered
with the various drafts of me imagining
another woman with my breast in her mouth
too satisfied to breathe.

IV. *Aliyyah says,*

Don't dodge being spoken.
The words that go in circles
will give up your cape and costume.
The way you shimmy can't be undone.
Don't swallow how we come together,
from the worth in ourselves,

cooling unmasked faces
to meet in plain conversation.

We grip each other like fire escapes.
This time don't eat grass not to tell of my hands.
This is not gutter—the grooves fit for tongues—
this is the pothole we lose our wheels in.

V. *Angel*

I prefer my tea with sugar
when I talk to you. You make
each minute an island where we,
crowned and carpeted by green,
sip Dragon Well from our palms.

I'm necklaced by your talk.
I want to exchange my body
for yours—
be the canary in your cage,
hum every note you give.

You may find it strange
I think this way, but I'm
readying myself to approach
the musical brew of my yeses,
my season fitting to spring.

VI. *Ieela, I'm your Grape Crush*

Yesterday was the day I never met her.
I know her by last name too.
She needs reasons not to return home.

She searches by candlelight the catacombs
of women's bodies, saying, *God left the key in one.*
I get carbonated looking at dates. She hasn't said yes
to being my girlfriend. I'm reason for her to stay.
Her answers: bagel pyramids, pies rotated so the better
sides show. She sips and the soda sighs, slices my sandwich

in half, takes the piece closest to the door.
Her backside is glorious—it's a fast to watch her go.

VII. *Tanisha*

For weeks now, I've arrived during her shifts
and avoided her eyes—eyes have a way of hooking.
I watch her hands perform tender surgeries,
cut lines where bleeding isn't a sign of parting.

Tonight it is her mouth, a cupboard—
unchipped, the cups open for alms.
Her neck I hold and drink from the cool
of her cheek and pour myself inside her.

VIII. *Carolina*

She sweeps the streetlight
from her hair, sticks it behind
her ear, says, *I came down
when I heard music in my pots.*

We lose our shadows, our
gauche footing to invitations
made when we're in treble.

I'm of age to consent

to what she is asking:
Yes, this is yes.
Upstairs in her apartment,
she fixes the bedding.
The sarong I unknot
one base at a time.

Her tattoo band of fish
in my coral. Through crowns,
their fins and tails propel.

I peel back her waves.
This is a holy day,
meals come after sundown.

In her shirt, her scent flags.
In my skin, her touch is
pledged—a believer.

Lady In the House: Kitchen Speeches

1.

Bitches,

I'm here, beautifully unadorned, my words pears.
I know your gardens, her bent-over back, her knees
in this earth, our mothers' hands.

I've been searching for one pure answer, one complete
thing to feed loss. Something grown for your mouths,
a recipe my pots don't refuse.

Laboring between the hard-between and not-a-break,
amiss in the atmosphere are mutated eves, we are
first-stage zombie.

We've put our purses on ground and when we dream
of fish, we don't want them pregnant. There is a snake
sucking your milk—you like it.

When nails are painted red, it's a certain suggestion:
put on your feathers and make thunder with your plow.
I may be over-ripened.

Spoiled because I was left to go soft. Willing yourself
from under the weight of too little admiration—
ladybugs, take up residence.

Roots get suffocated and we need broader reach.
In our small paradise tomatoes were city in taste.
Dirt so dry it was a dying kiss—love changes your want.

2.

Bitches,

After 25 years underwater, a town resurfaces.
It's first breath startles the wound.
The ruins we left are born again.

I've been told to starve them but there's no need.
Saying thank you to an abandoned face has no
bearing on her now.

You're a bone in her voice she pitched a long time
ago. I have jade and regrets and when I'm held
in a dark place, this body sarcophagus.

The excavation happening around me, it's grief—
ancient and never born—turns me sour,
feels of little good.

I wonder about these honeycombs,
these elegant divides. We all know
it takes a village to raise and kill a child.

Call them pollutants, I have proof we can
make clouds. From the snake below, I predict
the stones that lay our hearts down.

There is one road in; you must walk
through someone's living room to get out.
You're not standing alone, the radio tuned,

in your bedroom, to a yesteryear song.
You are affirmative in your dance—

forgotten vocabulary dug from the deep
pockets of your purse, sweetly and august.
Through the crack I witness you.

3.

Bitches,

Does this desire for unconditional love
inhale into us the butcher's breath?
Our appetites require more traps and labor.

I'm at the bus stop rubbing my curves
down so they can fit less vulnerably.
Once in the woods I feel the multiplying

effect of one voice, frogs opening portals
beneath a Shandy night when moss
has a private touch.

I watch all my mothers' hands to see
her capabilities, what she kneads into her care,
the seasonings dropped into fish stew.

What broth is worthy of her spoons?
What she cooks and what she loves
has nuanced mixologies.

At first the natives couldn't see the Columbus
ships, no language for what's before their eyes.
There are those hindsights for consideration.

You say, *I knew it in my gut* and the gut got
ignored and what is wounded and wise,

confident and sure, gets locked in a basement,
gets walked on all fours, gets internalization.
So many monkeys on our backs, you don't see
us no more.

4.

Bitches,

Small-tiny bugs, not ants, ate a 2-foot weed
to the dirt—imagine what they do to our babies?
The eggshells that remained, my grandma mixed

into the potting soil, her mother-in-laws grew sharp
tongues. Is anger a machine that eats the heart's lion,
leaves it in a cave to approximate in sheep's wool?

For every month of March,
regardless of how it's orchestrated,
a drumline that hurts.

I don't know what armories we've constructed
for all those arms estranged from their torsos—
a sign that soon you enter

A town of those who cannot pass from here.
This is not the same box that promises a VCR,
instead offers old news and expired coupons

to entertain our surprise that we don't get
what we pray for, that fantasy is altered
by the road—

what is given can be taken as not intended

Mashing Cookies

for Hedgebrook

Not all of us are lesbians on this island circled by orcas.
We've come because we've been nesting stories,
hollow voices that need time to season. We all need
to loot our minds for the woman who surrendered to wolves.

In the morning, on a breast of land, we wake our oak,
light wood in waterfall, air out the owl. At the nipple,
I encourage a woman to leave her captor, but first
she must mash cookies for her daughter's cake.

The chef told us on arrival, there's a bottomless pot
of cookies, and the other night, after glasses of red wine,
we reached the bottom. The conversation turned to G-spots
and female ejaculation and two or three of us can do it—

the 5-continent ear whistler says *Oh yeah*, and relishes;
the one who eats her bones has Googled for instruction;
the oldest who winks when she purses doesn't reveal her numbers—
the rest of us, a little sheepish, take our crooks and Tagalongs.

Pedal

Fire or live wire
I will stick my fork
in the socket and if
it frightens me enough,
I may not stick it again.

Along comes a lady
teeming with all
sorts of currents
I want to get my
hands on, and I
refuse to remember
the last time I got burnt.

It's not just scientists
who want hypotheses
answered. I will
figure how far
I can go without
crossing the line
or how the line
can be pushed
to lose its function.

It's the same woman.
I'm replaying the evening
in '96: rain mists
through the window screen,
autumn Brooklyn. Later
on the kitchen floor,
making out in the Village,
then a series of events
led her to gone.

Rewarded with likenesses
of the first love to soothe
my teenage grief—
fresh women delivered
at a time when I'm
in a relationship
without vases.
What can I do?

Hold her longer each
time we say good night,
move each kiss closer
to her lips? Text her good
morning and flirt in codes
I sometimes don't
know what I'm saying?

I want her
to be my citizen.
She is beautiful and
funny and flawed
and guarded and
beautiful, I know.

It's a matter of how
long I'm willing
to have my cake
without taste.
I'm not concerned.

The urge hasn't mastered.
I can sit with it,
let it call my name
in all kinds of ways
until cars are what I hear—
which drivers slow
on yellows, which
drivers burn.

Four Square

here	:	MA	open	:	Robin
here	:	LA	open	:	Annie
here	:	UT	open	:	Luna
here	:		open	:	Mary

the car breaks in the wettest city, and the dead didn't need to swim; when we sigh before the family-owned motel, she knows the motel and the uncle, partly in his passing—I'm ready to get on with life	tear back her bitter skin, her pulp sweet, and in due time she's in my notches; bored by loops in their albums, I step from their breasts, their promises and shortbreads—they puppet their purses, *Look, look at all the better-than*

break	:	story	breathe	:	apart
break	:	fish	walk	:	apart
break	:	tears	fall	:	apart
break	:	sense	always	:	

it wasn't fair I had the charge of our lives and it wasn't charge you didn't understand and it was this conversation I had alone each night and it was this dislike for questions—and sorry I answered with a terrible pushing fright	an identity gone, fingerprints washed and now waiting for this other-face to emerge— did we lie to keep ourselves interested? did we park in the heart's forgettable den? did we hunger untamed? did the lake freeze us without correction?

Queen

I'm waiting for you like waiting
for all the bottles to simultaneously
burst on the bottle tree. Together like
one distraught chord hardened in our
siamesed neck. Play me, but you rarely
press past the woman bored. You think
my universe has gone dim? It is hellish
bright if you're willing. You always doubt
what you pull up from the well. Water
now frightens you. Come take me to town
before I turn into a ladybug, spotted for
the years it took you to nurse your deuces.

Rooster

Your backside a cello I scratch strings down

to the body's divide. These three chords

have the juice to bleed—you're a native in

my war. My horn won't be evaded. These

mammies to your back—remember I'm your

daddy, not the rooster who pulled down your

pants under the bridge the science teacher flashed.

Say your pussy is as wet as mine. These inhales

let out an OM and let me in and it's the pleasure

of walking into air-conditioned megastores

after 100-degree heat—the whole body testifies

we are plugged into one magnanimous force.

Beechnut

Winter in the mountains, the beech twisted
into paper we could use. In that classic
way, seen on TV, wanting one day to be
that girl, you revealed your Swiss army knife
and the bark knew we would. Maybe we scared
away the owls who may have nested there. Our
initials traveled to heart, aged our presence
to diaphanous to shirr between thought and
sometimes we move on. What is sown is
resilient. Shells grow spines; the nut, a sweet
portion, hints close and it's how I come to understand
our touch. Woodwinds have memory.
I haven't advanced beyond "Twinkle, Twinkle
Little Star" and the tapping on the streetlamp was often
opposite notes. We engineered shepherds
to herd our swords—Oakland felt similar disharmony
and built a lake to meet the need for breath and matter.
Water finds scent and apology and people to beach
on its cusp. Reminds the heart there are summer
dresses to be worn, and twirling that happens in them.

Glass

Glass eye, glass heart, glass jar, in which we try and keep our flickering selves, all the light in us is sexual, a luminous persistence—a heaven or a hell. —Rebecca Seiferle

Carved Susie in a banana skirt, sea dollar, and winded instruments
collected in my pockets, Bach-dressed monkeys, tagged and used for study,
and the terrible feeling of someone betraying the way I stay preserved.

Discovered at three: a broom's bristle touch behind Easter dresses.
I'm without guilt. No need for truth or dare, dare or truth has no
strings on me—each one of us are souvenir globes, still or disturb,
sand and coladas of a vacation.

The problem with returning ex-girlfriends—their hands elsewhere.
To redeem herself, she comes like a hound, turns to watch my rage
brandish its mane. Before orgasm, before we're sentinels with tears—

No uncle, no cry in a room full of she and I.
Adulterous berry, sweet and so winter, writes her name,
a heart, then the first letter we learn—a weak epoxy's promise.

I direct her to lovers who are amenable, who'll afghan
on ice-queen nights and stroke along her grain.
I do this instead of admitting the cracks through me.

Closet Case

It's not hard to hold you, your cries
have shaken you, you seem freezing.
You've beaten the dog, her eyes are red,
hidden behind your guitar and frightened to bark.
You threaten to throw yourself from the ledge—
who will catch you?

No people on this sidewalk,
they're inside watching news, eating
Chinese food from the Chinese Restaurant.
Whoever's out will regard your flight
like the first sign of rain—
speed up and try to find an awning before it storms.

> *you shout you are stupid, look to accuse me*
> *of sharing the belief, no, stupid, you are not—yes,*
> *i am stupid. no, those things, you should not say.*

We are lovers. When climbing the last five steps,
screams from behind your locked door serrate.
Someone is beating you, robbing boxes of books,
your wallet you can never find. You're on your knees,
tugging your hair—snap your neck from your clavicle
then this room will hear my lullaby.

You I cannot wake in the morning
spent the night carving your own sunrise.
Red circle and rays of pink pucker,
your throat buckled your breath
when you saw it run to the carpet.
The towel was not enough bandage.
My fingers pressed on each line, afloat like carrion—

sticks and rotten bark that becomes of a failed escape.
You bled not to take you to the hospital.

> *i'm fucked up you shout, look to accuse the*
> *belief of sharing me. not fucked up, no you are.*
> *yes, so fucked I am. say those things, you*
> *shouldn't.*

The next time I will watch you,
clean the razor. Handcuff my hands to your wrists.
Breasts to back will pulse our sweat. Next time
your hands crave to cut—my fingers with the blade.

Craves

The words might as well be bar coasters,
mess in pockets detergent don't clean.
I encounter in myself an end.

What to do with empty legs, stillness
that consents to punishment?
I've been reckless.

You reveal undone seams after another,
your pain a burden of worms,
looking for unstormed ground.

I watch you like porn, pleasured
and disgusted by how much you wanted it.
Believed marriage would make us better.

I know this saga as my mother's daughter.
It's nice to toy a mouse
until its guts spill—I need to retract.

You're weathery over not getting
the hand-me-down way I love,
means your heart is unconditional.

Me not wanting to give
the hand-me-down way I love
means I apologize.

Like your mother's shot glasses,
there are things that distract
you from your abandonment—

I love the smell of mothballs
for the memory of my grandmother,
but it's her daughter who's in my closets.

Manly Shoes

Women in my family wear men's shoes. Tall, with feet past 11, they knew to walk into the haberdashery, find something practical, not too manly but could pass. At ten, I wasn't petite enough to be a girl—it would have been nice to play. Wore boy's jeans, medium shirts because the sleeves reached my wrists. Later, modeled my haircut after my mother's '70s natural, said thank you even when they called me sir.

You grew up pressed-and-curled; dresses, lady-like ma'ams and sirs; my brother made fun I was too much homeboy. Permitted to walk with dominion then switch, I can't keep roles. Stones are broken off from something larger. It's sad being removed from your greater self. Your breasts waterless when the binding's off. You're shy and insecure beneath underwear that would make your uncle and ex-boyfriend Marys if they touched again. In some moments we are kept, dressing in cures to save ourselves.

I had no boyfriends. Even in a uniform, acted like I was in jeans. We were young and I was unusual; they chose girls from the front of the line. I'd talk to her, the other tall girl. We got called Twin Towers—looked the same height until measured close. Her clothes smelled of Tide, and her pitcher's arm was often sore. Fixed her ponytail; brushed off loose hairs; found ways to touch, even if it meant removing lint.

I was taught, you break it—you pay for it. I'm cordial to the more of you exposed in dark. You came in pieces with unyielding guards. I was once warned: loving women come with them. I've managed myself into a dress in hopes to fix. Your F to M, pronoun shift, does nothing to break the scale that weighs and values. What will be rescued in becoming him?

I heard the boys say who could do good jobs; who they wanted in stairwell B. Saw girls fatigue from keeping defense, others complacent. I informed and interrupted, was told to mind my business. I step aside and you occupy your aloneness, falling quiet and welcoming the pleasure of peeling until bleeding the skin off your breast. You awaken into a stranger face to become a citizen of your own.

After Watching Obama Win His First Presidency, We Go See Tina Tuna

You take Anna Mae's stage name and make it fish.
Dressed in tulle and sparkle, in platform stilettos,
drag Tina, more masculine than her muscles can ever be,
into a river so queer the water maquillages our faces.

I'm a clap waiting to happen. Your hands, thick and brimming,
articulate the beat of our bodies meeting—the church wakes
in my chest, the choir quivers with Tina Turner's lips. Your mouth
around every note, without your baritone pouring into that hoarse hook

about breaking and staying. How do you not sink into song
until lyrics grin with your teeth? Between your hard cleavage, I slip
a five into the wailing aperture found in any woman's heart,
into the part of the sun we don't see as blue.

Seven Marys

Mary Mary Mary you cold thumb suckin
Lookin for you, but you keep duckin
I wanna find you, I gotta tell you somethin
So just be quiet and don't say nuttin
Mary Mary Mary why you out there stuntin?
Supposed to be with me, but now you're frontin
We started out new, you used to be true
Now you're buggin, what's wrong with you?

Mary, Mary WHY YA BUGGIN?
Mary, Mary I NEED YA HUGGIN

—"Mary Mary," RUN DMC

Mary R. E. D.

You have gone and so has my beauty and you
are my rejection, firm and as knowing as this
ground that cannot hold still. You said: *I've
imagined you dead.* So this death I've become.
I take the dirt and I'm least to martyr, but starve
myself organically. I'm spiritual in my suffering.
Died in you and in many others. Gone rigor mortis,
wandering where I've put myself to rest in pieces.

I'm no more alive than when you left. The phantom
pain of wanting my head each time Mercury retrogrades.
My sobs bring the effluvia of our memories to a dream.
I smell you like yesterday. Your outfit is far too fag to be
angelic. Your posture welcomes, and then I'm alarmed
into beating this heart without you. It's my hand against
my chest when it's realized hard truths come in brick form.

Mary O

Having sex during menses, in a bonded relationship,
is a very powerful way of sharing blood. Why do you
think there has been such a taboo? Why were you steered
away from the blood mysteries for eons? Perhaps because
it would open doors of knowledge that the gods did not wish
you to have. Blood contains the archives of personal, planetary,
and celestial experience. When blood is experienced in a sexual
union, you are flooded with waves of knowledge, much of it
beyond your present ability to understand and integrate.
     Eureka freeze, Marciniak puts "Shebang" before our brains,
and bless you. You've been marked on the neck and soles, too.
I have my same rituals: hot bath and cayenne tea, *Legally Blonde*
and OG Kush. Randy's warmed, you're strapped on. You set
a spell with your M-i-double s-i-double s-i-double p—I'm ludicrous
mayflies. We go toward streetlights, Shell signs, aim for fireworks, fanatic
for any moon, our lives risked for good intentions—doing-it in the middle
of the street. This is your house, Mary O, and your part in these curtains.

Yell, Mary

You walked off with my skin, I lit a candle. Your absence is one
long scarf and at the bull's eye of this concentric circling, I am.
Loving you was like trying to hold water, so I began to drink.

You wanted too what I wanted too and yet not us together.
Haunts me like the Hudson with a 7-thirty-seven on its tongue,
how silent I can be. Listen, the kitty in the crawl space is in heat.
It's unfair she can be vocal about her cunt, so lightning in her need.

You selected the sand for our hourglass, and when I flipped,
it was about time. I can do horrible things to your ego, grow
fingernails long and hard and unbreakable, put my initials in
your face. With every muscle, do you remember lifting my breast

and returning my heart to its cage? Your thumb imprinted
and blood travels its grooves and a ballad brings me to my window.
You were never so bold to love out loud. I can smell your ghost,
I solemnly swear, I promise not to dis you. The conflagration frees
these ashes to be radical in our cells.

Mary Don't-Grow-On-Trees

I shake this heart to get the last coin out, the last folded bill where
you wrote "Do Not Spend." My fear of being without is so rich, it
needs to be reminded that there is a dollar I can fall back on. I've
fallen, your hands catch in memory, and this concussion is my
trust in all things not there. The ground, however, doesn't reveal
your steps, has no attachment to your gait, even though there are
hips and shoulders that show your motion, men with faces that
is your face, staring for the green light, and the orange trees grow
the scent of our first meeting. When the missing inquires on your
whereabouts, I don't want to know where you are. You're a peculiar
bird and I've kept your blue feather. I parent this distance, which
is now about to enter the first grade, and she has your brown eyes. I
give her the soft and openness my love once lacked. Each time she
walks into those school doors, I wait for the bells to bring her back.

Mary Blue

You're my Bedfordstuyvesant, my bow and taboo,
I get ride or die with my arrow. All is petty bull
and pussy willows, your gravitas church Nina, *New
Moon Daughter*, Sadé is our hands' holla—*Purple
Rain*, sunshines, you hot damn grace and gracias!
Word to my Mother—like this, god is witness.
Baby baby baby please, baby please, baby baby please
let down your puzzle—bet: my verde chakra, your
buxom breath. Mark my Toms, I'll solve your 99
balloons. There's no going back from raw. New story
you, mezzo and wood bending. My love, you're the
darling dang—true-dat, true-dat, true—dat-dat-dat.

Mary, I

knew to put wings on all of who I was.
In a ritual of letting go, I burnt others—
the kitchen sink has a scorch mark.
Still this ache and its silent amplifications.
No one listens with your years.
Breakfast is not the ceremony it used to be,
with its toasts. Driving down the West Side
Highway, the city starts to rise, and two French
boys in the back, who later kiss on our balcony,
and just last summer the Towers were the skyline.
From full-size mermaids in fish tanks, we've
changed our Snoop to conservative volumes,
and quieted your holy spirit, but the finger-snap
could not be smoked.

Violet Mary

You are a cocoon I dare not break.
The struggle to live will free your beauty.
Who am I to interfere with your journey?
you said, with the hills going 60mph south,

and I remember where we were going. This house
by the riverside knew flood and bonfire and we made it.
We broke and knew ourselves to be a love rich, trees eat
off it. We do too—want grief as an artifact, an intimate
chaos to do good. I'm a woman grown better by my choices.

We could not see our bodies as easily as we thought.
Our darlings I bury to give them another life.
As sure as a bitch who breaks her chain,
this house knows a rainbow too.

Notes

"Tail" is the literal meaning for the Danish term "svans"; it's derogatory and used for men.

"Six Colors" is the literal meaning for the Haitian term "sis kouler."

"With Feathers" is the literal meaning for the derogatory Spanish (Puerto Rican) term "plumifero."

"Paw" is the literal meaning for the Dutch term "poot" and is derogatory.

"Auntie" is the literal meaning for the derogatory Slovene term "tetka" and French term "tata."

"Dagger" is the literal meaning for the highly derogatory Spanish (Mexican) term "puñal."

"Lilla, Inscribed": "lilla" is a derogatory Estonian term, used for men, and it's literal meaning is a diminutive of "flower."

"Gun(n)" is dedicated to 15-year-old Sakia Gunn, who was murdered for being gay in Newark, New Jersey, in May 2003. "Gun" is the literal meaning for the Danish term "bøsse"; it is neutral and used for men.

"Blue Boy" is the literal meaning for the Latvian term "zilais," and is derogatory and used for men.

"Bat" is the literal meaning for the Finnish term "lepakko," slightly derogatory, and used for lesbians.

"Whole Lot of Lot" references Lot's people of Sodom and

Gomorrah. The phrase "Texan Byrd" refers to James Byrd, Jr., who was murdered in Jasper, Texas, in 1998, by three men who tied a chain around his neck, hitched him to the back of a pick-up truck, and dragged him more than three miles to his death.

"Warm Water" references the highly derogatory Slovene term "toplovodar," which means "warm-water person."

"Comrades" is the literal meaning for the Mandarin term "tóngshì" and is a pun on the Communist usage of the word; it is neutral.

"Little Deer" (a twinky bottom) is the literal meaning for Portuguese term "veadinho" and is neutral or derogatory.

"Hold Your Part of A Deal" references the Romanian term "bulangiu," which is from "bulan," police stick, and also means "one that does not hold his part of a deal." It is derogatory.

"Kokobar" was the first cybercafé owned and operated by African American women, located in the Fort Greene neighborhood of Brooklyn, New York. It was co-founded by angel Kyodo williams and Rebecca Walker in 1996.

"Mashing Cookies" is the literal meaning for the Portuguese term "bate-biscoito" and is slightly derogatory and somewhat neutral.

"Pedal" is the literal meaning for the Polish term "pedał" and is derogatory.

"Four Square" is a ball game played among four players on a square court divided into quadrants. Each player occupies a quadrant, and the ball is bounced between players. The object of the game is to eliminate players in the highest squares, so you can advance to their ranking.

"Torn" is the literal meaning for the Portuguese term "roto," and is derogatory.

"Rooster" is the literal meaning for the Lithuanian term "gaidys"; it is derogatory and also used for the lowest caste of prisoners.

"Beechnut" is the literal meaning for the Czech term "bukvice" and is slightly derogatory.

"Glass" is the literal meaning for Mandarin term "bōlí" and is derogatory.

"Closet Case" is the literal meaning for the Portuguese term "enrustido" and is derogatory.

"Craves" comes from a neutral Inuktitut term that means "male-male and female-female who has a crav[ing] or lust."

"Manly Shoes" references the derogatory Portuguese lesbian term "sapatão," which means "huge manly shoes."

"Seven Marys": in both Spanish and Catalan there are several derogatory alterations of "Mary" that mean gay.

"Mary O": The opening stanza is a quotation from the chapter "Galvanization of the Goddess" from the book *Earth: Pleiadian Keys to the Living Library* by Barbara Marciniak.

Acknowledgements

I'm grateful for the following publications that have published versions of the poems in this collection:

"Paw," "Strangers," "Glass," and "Craves," and "Lady in the House: Kitchen Speeches" ("lady in the boat"), *Adrienne: A Poetry Journal of Queer Women*, Issue 2; "After Watching Obama Win His First Presidency, We Go See Tina Tuna," *Bat City Review*, Issue 12; "Dirty Fruit," *Cave Canem Anthology XII: Poems 2008-2009*, Willow Books; "Dagger," *Collective Brightness*, Sibling Rivalry Press; "Pedal," *Eleven Eleven*, Issue 17; "Effluvium" (excerpts), *Fingernails Across the Chalkboard: Poetry and Prose on HIV/AIDS from the Black Diaspora*, Third World Press; "Four Square," *inter|rupture*; "Drag Up," *Knocking at the Door: Poems About Approaching the Other*, Write Bloody Publishing; "Beechnut," *Lambda Literary*; "Little Deer" and "Torn," *The New Sound: A Journal of Interdisciplinary Art & Literature*, Spring 2012; "Kokobar," "Mashing Cookies," "Rooster," and "Closet Case," *PANK Magazine* online; "Tail," *Prairie Schooner*, Winter 2015; "Trip the Light Fantastic," *The San Francisco Bay Guardian*, Vol. 44.38; "Blue Boy," *Strange Machine*; "Gun(n)" and "Passing," *Street Lit Anthology*, Scarecrow Press; "Queen," ("I'm waiting for you like waiting"), *Your Impossible Voice*, Issue 1; "Chance Is Based On True Events," *Word Riot*, September 2010.

And big-love thank-yous to the following organizations and individuals for their support, encouragement, being, and inspiration:

Augury Books and Kate Angus, Atlantic Center for the Arts, Cave Canem Foundation, the Center for Women Writers at Salem College, Goddard College, Hedgebrook, Juniper Summer Writing Institute, and the MFA for Poets & Writers at UMass, Amherst.

Kazim Ali, Ross Gay, Roxane Gay, Jewelle Gomez, Daniel Handler, Amy King , Tracie Morris, Willie Perdomo, and Pamela Sneed.

Aliyyah Abdur-Rahman, Dawn Wisteria Bates, Michelle Belisle, Joy Brown, Gloria Carter, S.C. Carter, Heather Christle, Katherine Chua, Geimy Colon, Theresa Coulter, Natalie Diaz, Kari Donatelli, R. Erica Doyle, Jana Fleishman, Laurie Foos, Soma Mei Sheng Frazier, Jess Finck, Nigel Golding, Shaquana Golding, Uriah Golding, Matthew Goodman, Ieela Grant, Yvonne Grimes, Nila Grutman, Minal Hajratwala, Sulay Hernandez, Herukhuti, Sir Woofum Jackson, Jessica Jones, Monica Juarbe, Stephanie Kallos, Robin Coste Lewis, Kenyetta Lovings, Sarah Lapido Manyika, Jenny Martin, Cate Marvin, Darrell Gane McCalla, Amber McZeal, Ebony Meeks, Rosebud Ben Oni, Shelagh Patterson, David Robinson, Lee Ann Roripaugh, Kwame A. Ross, Serena Reed, Metta Sáma, Ibert Schultz, Kayana Schultz, Muriel Shockley, Rebecca Seiferle, Roger Guenveur Smith, Janet Sylvester, Anastacia Tolbert, Donald Washington, Diana Waters, Carolina Wheat, Cate White, Denise White, Jamar White, Dara Wier, angel Kyodo williams, and Mary Sui Yee Wong.

As always, deep gratitude and appreciation for my immediate and extended family and to my loving wife Samantha Florio.

About the Author

Arisa White is a Cave Canem fellow, an MFA graduate from the University of Massachusetts, Amherst, the author of the chapbooks *Black Pearl* and *Post Pardon*, the second of which was adapted into an opera, as well as the full-length collections *Hurrah's Nest* and *A Penny Saved*. Arisa has received residencies, fellowships, or scholarships from Headlands Center for the Arts, Port Townsend Writers' Conference, Rose O'Neill Literary House, Squaw Valley Community of Writers, Hedgebrook, Atlantic Center for the Arts, Prague Summer Program, Fine Arts Work Center, and Bread Loaf Writers' Conference. She is a 2013-2014 recipient of an Investing in Artists grant from the Center for Cultural Innovation and a BFA faculty advisor at Goddard College in Vermont.

arisawhite.com

Made in the USA
Charleston, SC
07 February 2017